GW0036l847

CONTENTS

THE FOLD-OUT PANORAMA

THE PYRAMID BUILDERS OF THE WORLD

THE pyramids of Egypt and the Americas are among the greatest buildings ever constructed by the human race. Pyramids were built in different lands by different peoples – for different reasons, at different times. On the desert sands of Egypt and in the jungle clearings in South America, many of these mighty stone mountains can still be seen to this day. Why were they built?

The story behind the Egyptian pyramids and their builders is not exactly the same as the story behind the pyramids of the native people of South America and Mexico, but there are similarities.

The jagged pyramids of Tikal rise up from the Mexican rainforest. They were built by the Maya in the 8th century A.D.

Wherever they were built, pyramids were the works of people capable of organizing human labor on a giant scale. They were the works of skilled craftsmen who used simple tools and equipment, people who lacked the means of transportation and power machinery we call essential today. They were the creations of people who were commanded to work by all-powerful rulers, and they were built not just to please the king or to provide him with a tomb, but for religious reasons. Strange, sometimes cruel gods played a role in the building of the pyramids. Today, although the builders and their gods are gone, the pyramids remain.

The pyramids of Giza, near Cairo, Egypt, were built between 2660 and 2560 B.C.

THE PYRAMIDS OF ANCIENT EGYPT

THE pyramids were built as tombs, or burial places, for the pharaohs, the powerful god-kings of Egypt.

They were designed to allow the king's soul to climb up to the sky to join the sun god – and then to come down again to his tomb when he wanted. The angles of the pyramids were meant to symbolize the slanting rays of the sun.

The Step Pyramid (ABOVE) was built by the architect Imhotep as a tomb for King Zoser at Saqqara, just south of Giza. Made entirely of limestone, it is 200 feet high.

Pharaohs (BELOW) were buried with treasures for use in the afterlife, including models of furniture, weapons, and ships.

Pyramid design took some time to develop. The first pyramid, built some time between 2800 and 2700 B.C., had stepped sides, like a giant stairway. A hundred years later, smooth-sided pyramids made an appearance. The first kind of smooth-sided pyramids were built for King Snefru, who ruled about 2670 B.C. They were stepped pyramids with the sides filled in to make continuous slopes.

The Great Pyramid of Giza belonged to Cheops. It was 481 feet high and was built using about 2.5 million blocks of stone.

The first true smooth-sided pyramids were the pyramids at Giza. They set the pattern for a thousand years. Today, about 87 pyramids survive in the world, though not all are as well-preserved as the Great Pyramid of Cheops.

Pyramid building came to an end about 1650 B.C. This was probably because the pyramids had been plundered so often. Standing out like stone mountains in the landscape, they were an easy target for robbers.

THE GIFT OF THE NILE

Hapy was the spirit of the Nile. The Egyptians believed that he poured the annual flood waters out of his waterpot.

MUCH of Egypt is desert. It would be a harsh, impossible environment for people to live in if it were not for one very important feature in the Egyptian landscape – the river Nile.

The Nile provides Egypt with life. Every year, after heavy rains to the south in tropical Africa, the Nile floods its banks. At the time of the pharaohs, before the building of great dams, this flood spread all the way up the Nile. It left a rich, black

The rich soil left after the Nile flooded allowed the Egyptians to grow grain, cereals, flax, and vegetables.

layer of mud, just right for growing crops. Farming, and the food supply, depended on this annual flood, which began every year around June 15th. To make the most of flood waters, the Egyptians built canals, dikes, and irrigation channels.

The Egyptians understood the vital part the Nile played in their lives. They thought of their country as "a gift of the Nile," and the Nile itself as the center of the world.

...ore the sun. By ...ies, the astronomers d p.c.. when the flood was going to happen.

THE PYRAMID SOCIETY

As a symbol of their power, pharaohs wore the Red Crown of the Delta and the white Crown of Upper Egypt. The Blue Crown was a war helmet.

PHARAOH POWER

In very ancient times, about 3000 B.C., anyone who touched the pharaoh – even accidentally – could be instantly put to death.

IN the days of the pyramid builders, society itself was organized rather like a pyramid. The great base of the social pyramid were the poorest groups, the peasants and laborers. Then came the merchants and skilled classes – scribes, artists, craftsmen, and priests. In the wealthiest, most powerful groups were the nobility, the leaders of the priesthood, and the army. At the top of the pyramid was the all-powerful god-king, the pharaoh. (Pharaoh comes from the Egyptian *per-o*, meaning "great house.")

The priests, scribes, soldiers, and landowners carried out the demands and wishes of the pharaoh, but it was the peasants who did all the hard work. They farmed the land and provided most of the work force to build the great tombs, temples, and pyramids. Foreign prisoners of war, used as slave labor, worked with the peasants.

Although rigid, Egyptian society was fair. Bread and beer were considered basic rights, and when famine struck, the grain stores were opened up to all.

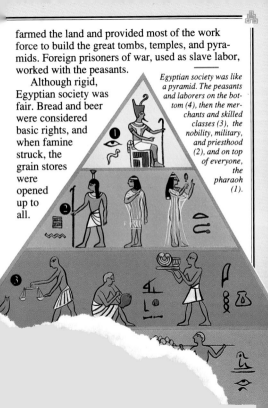

Egyptian society was like a pyramid. The peasants and laborers on the bottom (4), then the merchants and skilled classes (3), the nobility, military, and priesthood (2), and on top of everyone, the pharaoh (1).

SCRIBES, STAR-GAZERS, AND HEALERS

A VERY important section of Egyptian society was made up of the professionals – scribes, doctors, and astronomers. Ancient Egyptian wisdom in medicine, mathematics, geometry, engineering, and astronomy was widely respected.

Scribes were always shown holding their papyrus scroll.

These subjects often developed out of practical use. Geometry was important in pyramid building – the 52° incline of the sloping walls had to be precisely calculated. Medical knowledge of the body and its organs increased because of the practice of mummification.

The Egyptians were especially interested in the study of the stars. The country depended on the annual flooding of the Nile, which always happened when the bright Dog Star, Sirius (which the Egyptians called *Sothis*), rose in the eastern dawn just bef̶ ̶ ̶ ̶ observing the sk̶ ̶ ̶ ̶ coul̶d̶ ̶p̶r̶e̶d̶i̶ ̶ ̶

SIGN WRITING

Hieroglyphic writing uses pictures. To represent a fish, a scribe would simply draw a fish. But hieroglyphs could also stand for a consonant: a drawing of a mouth, for example, also meant an "r." In this way, hieroglyphs made up a kind of alphabet, but with consonants only – vowels were not used.

Watching the regular movements of stars also helped them to make an accurate calendar.

Writing was important in ancient Egypt, as a great deal of paperwork was needed to administer Egypt's complicated rules and regulations. Scribes used reed brushes and *papyrus*, paper made from pulped papyrus reeds.

It was an honor and a privilege to be a scribe. Scribes also acted as accountants, lawyers, and tax collectors – but did not have to pay any taxes themselves.

ETERNAL LIFE

Tomb paintings were meant to cheer and entertain the dead in the afterlife. This is a portrait of the wife of Nebamun, a nobleman, from a wall painting in his tomb.

THE Egyptians believed that a person would live forever if the body was preserved after death. In very ancient times, only the pharaoh was expected to live forever, and be reborn after death like the Egyptian god *Osiris*. Later, people began to believe that anyone could share this endless future. They were sure that life after death would be just like their earthly life.

These beliefs meant that great efforts were made to preserve the body after death, and to keep it safe. To do

The mummified body was laid in a decorated wooden coffin called a sarcophagus. This one belonged to Tutankhamun.

this, the dead body was first mummified. The internal organs were removed and stored in special jars. Then the body was treated with special oils, resins, chemicals, and salt – and left to dry for 70 days. After that, the mummy was washed, wrapped in gauze bandages, and coated with scented gum. Then it was buried – for the pharaoh and his courtiers, it was a costly and dazzling business.

After death, the jackal-headed god, Anubis, *weighed the heart of the dead person against the feather of* Maa't, *the goddess of Truth and Justice.*

CANOPIC JARS

When the liver, lungs, stomach, and intestines had been removed from the dead body, they were stored separately in alabaster pots called canopic jars. Stoppers were carved to represent the heads of the four Sons of *Horus,* each responsible for one organ. They were *Amset* (human-headed), *Hapi* (baboon-headed), *Duametef* (dog-headed), and *Qebehsenuf* (falcon-headed).

THE PYRAMID BUILDERS AT WORK

As soon as a pharaoh came to power in ancient Egypt, his thoughts turned to one very important project: the building of a tomb to protect his body after death. Many pharaohs chose pyramids to mark their tombs.

Vast numbers of laborers and craftsmen were immediately set to work. First, the site was prepared and leveled. Large blocks of stone were brought along the Nile by barge to the construction site. Once unloaded, they were dragged on sleds along a wooden pathway built on the desert sand. Armies of masons prepared the stones so they would fit together neatly. To raise heavy blocks, as the pyramid grew, ramps were built against the

> ### WHAT'S IN A NAME?
>
> The Egyptian word for pyramid is *mer*. The Greeks invented the nickname "pyramids," which comes from their word *pyramis*, a kind of wheat cake.

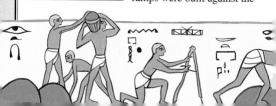

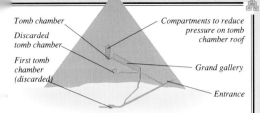

Tomb chamber

Discarded tomb chamber

First tomb chamber (discarded)

Compartments to reduce pressure on tomb chamber roof

Grand gallery

Entrance

Cross section of the Great Pyramid of Cheops, showing tomb chambers, some of which were not used.

pyramid faces. The heavy work was done by peasants and slave labor forces during the flood season when it was impossible to farm. Pyramid building was a long process. Work on the Great Pyramid of Cheops lasted over 30 years.

Inside the tomb chamber of the pyramid, artists and sculptors produced magnificent paintings, carvings, and statues of the gods and the tomb's owner. The god Osiris was often shown watching, as the jackal-headed god, Anubis, brought the dead person before him for the judgment ceremony.

FAMOUS PHARAOHS

EGYPTIANS believed that pharaoh was the son of the sun god, and that when he died he would join the sun god and sail with him in a boat across the skies each day.

Not all the pharaohs built pyramids. After 1650 B.C., elaborate non-pyramid tombs were built, many in the Valley of the Kings. Other pharaohs are commemorated by temples, huge statues called colossi, and obelisks.

SNEFRU (C. 2700 B.C.) was the owner of two – possibly three – pyramids. He was a powerful and benevolent king. It is said that he talked directly to ordinary people, often calling them "friend" or "comrade."

The obelisk of Seti I, which stands in Rome today.

CHEPHREN (C. 2620 B.C.) was the son or possibly brother of Cheops. He built the second largest of all the pyramids at Giza. The Great Sphinx was built by his sculptors.

Mummy mask found in the tomb of Tutankhamun.

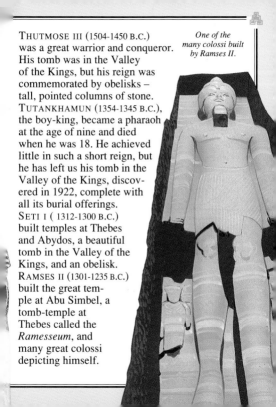

THUTMOSE III (1504-1450 B.C.) was a great warrior and conqueror. His tomb was in the Valley of the Kings, but his reign was commemorated by obelisks – tall, pointed columns of stone.

TUTANKHAMUN (1354-1345 B.C.), the boy-king, became a pharaoh at the age of nine and died when he was 18. He achieved little in such a short reign, but he has left us his tomb in the Valley of the Kings, discovered in 1922, complete with all its burial offerings.

SETI I (1312-1300 B.C.) built temples at Thebes and Abydos, a beautiful tomb in the Valley of the Kings, and an obelisk.

RAMSES II (1301-1235 B.C.) built the great temple at Abu Simbel, a tomb-temple at Thebes called the *Ramesseum*, and many great colossi depicting himself.

One of the many colossi built by Ramses II.

THE PYRAMIDS OF THE AMERICAS

Duﬁﬁﬁ the early 16th century, European settlers and Spanish conquistadors – explorers greedy for gold – first set foot in the Americas. The age-old way of life of the pyramid builders of the Americas was suddenly brought into contact with a modern world, which destroyed it.

More than 1,000 years before Christ, the building of temple-pyramids had been important. The Olmecs built altars to their gods, raising them up on great earthen mounds.

This pattern of a temple mound was then copied in stone by various peoples. Over many centuries, the Maya built temple-pyramids at Tikal, Palenque, and Chichen Itza.

In Teotihuacan, northeast of Mexico City, the great "Pyramid of the

Hernando Cortes (1485-1547) conquered Mexico in 1521 and brought an end to the Aztec Empire.

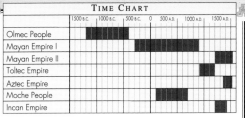

Sun" was built around 150 A.D., but no one knows by whom. In the 11th or 12th century, the Toltec people built a great four-tiered temple-pyramid at Tula, northwest of Mexico City. During their short but glorious empire, the Aztecs built the mighty double pyramid in their city of Tenochtitlan. And in Peru, the Moche people built twin *adobe* (sun-dried brick) pyramids at Moche. Centuries later, the Incas built the Sun Temple at Coricancha in Cuzco, and the shrine at Pachacamac, near Lima.

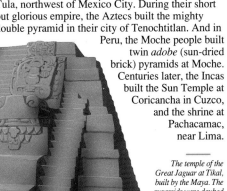

The temple of the Great Jaguar at Tikal, built by the Maya. The pyramids were daubed with red paint, which has now faded away.

LIFE IN A HARSH LAND

THE struggle to grow food in the rugged landscape of rainforest, steep mountains, volcanos, and earthquakes was hard. Peru, for example, where the Moche and the Inca people lived, was a land of many contrasts, from the coast and barren desert, to the high Andes and snowy mountains with the jungle and the Amazon basin behind.

In Peru and central Mexico, maize – Indian corn – was grown from c. 1200 B.C. It was sometimes called "food of the gods."

Skill and adaptability were needed to make the best of this landscape. To add to the amount of flat farming land, special terraced fields with stone walls were built in the slopes of the mountains. Terraced fields were made by cutting wide steps into the mountainside and then leveling them off. Providing water for the

---

THE DRINK OF THE GODS?

Cacao beans were ground up and mixed with water to make a drink. This drink was offered to the gods during ritual worship. The Aztecs called it *chocolatl* ("bitter water"), and when the Spanish took cacao back to Europe, they took the name as well – chocolate.

A map of present-day Mexico and Peru shows where three ancient civilizations developed.

☐ Aztec

■ Maya

☐ Inca

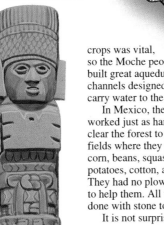

A statue of the Toltec god of rain shows how fierce the people believed the gods to be.

crops was vital, so the Moche people built great aqueducts, channels designed to carry water to the fields.

In Mexico, the Maya worked just as hard to clear the forest to make fields where they grew corn, beans, squashes, sweet potatoes, cotton, and cacao. They had no plows or animals to help them. All the work was done with stone tools.

It is not surprising that the gods these people worshiped and made sacrifices to were mostly gods of rain, sun, water, and plants.

Jaguar-Knights,
Priests, and Emperors

T HE pyramid builders of the Americas created many different kinds of societies. The Maya had the longest lasting and most cultured civilization, being the only Amerindians to develop a written language. Each Mayan city was an independent city-state, with a single ruler.

In Peru and in Mexico, two very powerful groups rose up, conquered their neighbors, and created magnificent empires. The empire-builders of Mexico were the Aztecs. In Peru, the Incas seized power.

At the height of its power, the Aztec Empire

The Aztec army was led by three important groups of warriors – Jaguar-knights (LEFT), Arrow-knights, and Eagle-knights. They wore carved wooden helmets and costumes made from animal skins or feathers. For the Maya, the serpent (RIGHT) was the symbol of great sacred power and was used by priests and emperors alike.

ruled 10 million people. This success was due to a large, well-organized army. The Aztecs believed that war was the proper occupation of men, and fought battles constantly, either to gain territory or to capture prisoners to sacrifice to the gods. All boys were trained as soldiers, unless they were to be priests. The Aztec emperor, who commanded the army, belonged to the Royal house. He did not inherit the throne automatically; he was chosen by a special committee of priests, soldiers, and noblemen.

Each Mayan city-state had an emperor. He was thought to be descended from a god. When the ruler died, the crown passed to the eldest son.

The Inca people were also ruled by an emperor, the *Sapa Inca*. Like the pharaohs of Egypt, he was thought to be a sun god, and had total power. Incan society was rigid and well-organized. The common people had to spend some part of the year working for the emperor, either farming, building, or serving in the army. This duty was called *mit'a*.

SUN, MOON, AND STARS

The double-headed serpent was a powerful religious symbol to the Aztecs. It signified strength, skill, and wisdom.

THE religious beliefs of the pyramid builders were closely bound up with the harsh landscape they lived in. The sun was the chief god in most cultures, and all sky gods were very important. The pyramids were to lift the temples so that the priests could be nearer to the gods.

The chief sun god of the Incas was *Viracocha.* He was the creator of all things. Coricancha, the great temple-pyramid at Cuzco, was dedicated to the sun. The Incas also worshiped other sky gods: a thunder god, the moon god, and star gods.

The peoples of central Mexico had their own gods. Like the Incas, many showed their fear of the power of the natural world. The Maya worshiped gods of the sky and earth. They believed that everybody descended from the moon "mother"

The Temple of Niches, built by the Maya at Tijuana. Each niche represented a day in the Mayan year.

and the sun "father." The Aztecs, too, worshiped gods like these. At their famous temple-pyramid in the city of Tenochtitlan, they worshiped *Huitzilopochtli*, the god of sun and war, and *Tlaloc*, the god of rain.

Constantly studying the stars in their high temples, the priests became expert astronomers. They could tell the time of year by the position of the sun, moon, and stars in the sky.

SKY CALENDARS

The Mayan priests used their knowledge of the stars to make two extremely complicated and accurate calendars. One was for everyday use, and was based on a 365-day year (divided into 18 months of 20 days, with five days left over). The other was a sacred calendar, 260 days long, with 13 weeks of 20 days. Only the priests were allowed to use this, as it foretold the future.

SACRIFICE

The sacrificial altar, often shaped like a jaguar, where the victim was ritually killed.

THE pyramid builders believed that the gods had to be offered sacrifices or gifts. Without sacrifices, they feared that the gods would become angry, and punish them. The rain god would refuse to send rain, the sun god would give no light – and people and their crops would be destroyed.

Sacrifices could be many things – animals, special jewelry, or money. But the Aztecs believed that *Huitzilopochtli*, god of sun and war, demanded the greatest of all sacrifices – human life, and blood.

Although the Maya also made human sacrifices, they were not as bloodthirsty as the Aztecs. Aztec warriors brought back prisoners from the battlefield especially to be sacrificed to *Huitzilopochtli*.

An engraved plate showing a priest cutting the heart out from the sacrificial victim.

For the Aztecs, war, farming, and religion were part of one great pattern. After the harvest, it was time to go to war. Then it was time for captives to be killed at the temple, then time to plant new crops. Then came another important religious festival – the Feast of the Flaying of Men, when more captives were skinned alive, and their hearts offered to the great sun god.

The Pyramid of the Sun at Tenochtitlan. Sacrificial ceremonies took place in front of the temple.

BUILDING THE TEMPLE-PYRAMIDS

Pyramid building demanded great organization and skill. The pyramids were truly massive. The temple-pyramid of the Giant Jaguar at Tikal, built by the Maya, comprised half a million cubic feet of rock. The pyramid at Cholula, built by the Toltecs, was even larger than the Great Pyramid of Cheops.

The building called for many workers, from quarrymen and laborers, to master-masons and artists. Blocks of stone were hewn from the quarries without

> **TEMPLE TITLE**
> The Aztecs called their temple-pyramids *teocallis*.

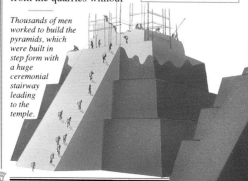

Thousands of men worked to build the pyramids, which were built in step form with a huge ceremonial stairway leading to the temple.

using metal tools. Archaeologists think this was done by boring holes into the rock, fitting wooden wedges into the holes, and soaking them with water. The water made the wood swell, and split the rock. From the quarry, the stone was carried to its destination on rollers and cables. Amerindians did not use the wheel for transportation, and did not have animals which could be used to pull heavy loads.

The pyramids were usually built by piling rubble onto existing mounds and facing it with stones. The temples were solid stone.

Once on site, the stones were shaped so that they fit together perfectly without mortar. There were no gaps between the stones.

The Incas were particularly skilled at wall-building. Their masons used hammers and bronze chisels. The pyramids were probably built by piling stones on top of existing tombs or temples. Once built, the temple-pyramids needed constant attention. In Tenochtitlan, thousands of Aztec craftsmen were employed to look after the temples.

THE EMPEROR GODS

THE emperors who ruled the Maya, Aztecs, and Inca did not build the temples to glorify themselves, although sometimes rulers were buried under or near a temple mound. The pyramids were for the worship of gods, and for ritual sacrifice.

The plumed headdress worn by Mayan emperors at great ceremonies.

One of the greatest Mayan emperors was PACAL (605-683), the builder of Palenque, one of the most powerful of all the Mayan city-states. Pacal built the Temple of the Sun, the Royal Palace, and the nine-tiered Temple of Inscriptions, which housed his tomb.

An ornate tumi knife used by priests in Incan ceremonies.

The story of MONTEZUMA II (1466-1520), last emperor of the Aztecs, began with the arrival of strangers in Mexico in 1519. These white men, riding horses and carrying strange weapons, were in fact Hernando Cortes and his band of Spanish conquistadors. The Aztecs believed that Cortes was the white god *Quetzalcoatl*, returning to them after many years away at sea. Montezuma sent gifts; in return he was kidnapped, imprisoned, and later killed in the fight to free him.

PACHACUTI (1438-1471), an Incan emperor, led many war expeditions and helped to mold the conquered land into part of the Incan Empire. He had two great gold images made for the Sun Temple, Coricancha, and designed the great capital, Cuzco.

ATAHUALPA (1525-1533) was the last great emperor of the Incas. When the Spaniard Francisco Pizarro (c. 1478-1541) landed in Peru, he captured Atahualpa, made him pay a huge ransom, forced him to become a Christian, and then had him executed. This was the cruel end of the mighty Incan Empire.

IMMORTAL INCAS

Like the Egyptian pharaohs, the Sapa Incas were preserved as mummies after their death. However, they were not buried. They were carried in ceremonial processions at Incan festivals.

An Incan gold ceremonial mask from Cuzco.

PYRAMID GODS

THE urge to get nearer to the gods was one of the reasons for building pyramids. The Egyptians and the South American peoples, particularly the Aztecs, had many gods and creation myths. Listed below is a selection of the most important gods worshiped by the Egyptians and the Aztecs.

EGYPTIAN GODS

OSIRIS – God of the Afterlife and Underworld
ISIS – Sister and wife to Osiris; goddess of the Earth
HORUS – Son of Osiris and Isis; god of Light and Heaven
ANUBIS – God of the Dead and Funerals
THOTH – God of Writing and Wisdom
SET – God of the Sky
RE or RA – God of the Sun

AZTEC GODS

QUETZALCOATL – The Plumed Serpent; god of Wisdom, Priesthood, and Learning
COATLICUE – Goddess of the Earth
CHALCHIUHTLICUE – Goddess of Running Water and Streams

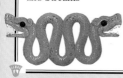

TEZCATLIPOCA – God of Wind and Magic
XIPE TOTEC – God of Vegetation and Renewal
XIUHTECUHTLI – God of Fire

A RUNNING PRESS / QUARTO BOOK
Joint copyright © 1993 Running Press / Quarto Publishing plc
Printed in China. All rights reserved under the Pan-American and
International Copyright Conventions.

Canadian representatives:
General Publishing Co., Ltd.,
30 Lesmill Road, Don Mills, Ontario M3B 2T6.

International representatives:
Worldwide Media Services, Inc.,
30 Montgomery Street,
Jersey City, New Jersey 07302.

9 8 7 6 5 4 3 2 1

Digit on the right indicates the number of this printing.

Library of Congress
Cataloging-in-Publication Number 93-83585

ISBN 1-56138-322-8

Designed by PETER BRIDGEWATER/ANNIE MOSS
Edited by VIV CROOT
Illustrated by TONY MASERO
Typeset by VANESSA GOOD

*This book may be ordered by mail from the publisher.
Please add $2.50 for postage and handling.
But try your bookstore first!*

RUNNING PRESS BOOK PUBLISHERS
125 South Twenty-second Street
Philadelphia, Pennsylvania 19103

WRITTEN BY SARAH HOWARTH

THE FOLD-OUT PANORAMA

The fold-out panoramic chart opposite divides into two parts. The first side shows how and why pyramids were built in Egypt, what happened when a pharaoh died and his body was taken to the pyramids, and why the pyramids went out of use. The second side takes a closer look at the life and customs of the people of the Aztec Empire of Mexico, and shows how they built and used the many temple-pyramids in their great capital city of Tenochtitlan.